ERNEST HEMINGWAY
ON WRITING

edited by

LARRY W. PHILLIPS

Scribner

New York   London   Toronto   Sydney

Scribner
1230 Avenue of the Americas
New York, NY 10020

Copyright © 1984 by Larry W. Phillips and
Mary Welsh Hemingway
All rights reserved,
including the right of reproduction
in whole or in part in any form.

First Scribner trade paperback edition 2004

Scribner and design are trademarks of Macmillan Library
Reference USA, Inc., used under license by Simon & Schuster,
the publisher of this work.

For information about special discounts for bulk purchases,
please contact Simon & Schuster Special Sales:
1-800-456-6798 or business@simonandschuster.com

Manufactured in the United States of America
10 9 8 7

Library of Congress Cataloging-in-Publication Data
Hemingway, Ernest, 1899–1961.

  Ernest Hemingway on writing.
    1. Hemingway, Ernest, 1899–1961—Quotations.
2. Fiction—Authorship—Quotations, maxims, etc.
I. Phillips, Larry W.   II. Title
PS3515.E37A6   1984   813'.52   84-5583
ISBN 0-684-18119-3
      0-684-85429-5 (Pbk)

Page numbers cited are from the Scribner paperback editions of
Hemingway's works.

This book is dedicated to my Mother and Father; to Mr. Edwin Benish; and to Charles ("Pete") Redfield of the Silver Coach.

Acknowledgments

The editor and the publisher gratefully acknowledge the
permission to reprint granted by the following authors and
publishers:

Mary Welsh Hemingway, for A Moveable Feast; By-Line:
Ernest Hemingway; Death in the Afternoon; Green Hills of
Africa; The Nick Adams Stories; Ernest Hemingway: Selected
Letters; Ernest Hemingway's Nobel Prize acceptance speech;
and one unpublished manuscript. All quotations from the works
of Ernest Hemingway are fully protected by copyright and are
used by permission.

Mary Hemingway and Alfred A. Knopf, Inc., for How It Was
by Mary Welsh Hemingway. Copyright © 1951, 1956, 1963,
1965, 1976 by Mary Welsh Hemingway.

George Plimpton, for "An Interview with Ernest Hemingway"
from The Paris Review 18 (Spring 1958).

Contents

Foreword

ERNEST Hemingway's public image as war correspondent, big-game hunter, and deep-sea fisherman has tended to obscure his lifelong dedication to the art of writing. Only those who knew him well realized the extent of that commitment. To Hemingway, every other pursuit, however appealing, took second place to his career as a writer. Underneath his well-known braggadocio, he remained an artist wholly committed to the craft. At some times he showed an almost superstitious reluctance to talk about writing, seeming fearful that saying too much might have an inhibiting effect on his muse.

But at other times, when he was not caught up in the difficulties of a new work, he was willing to converse freely about theories on the art of writing, and even his own writing methods. He did this often enough in his letters and other writings to make it possible to assemble this little book.

For readers of Hemingway who would like to know more about his aims and principles as a writer, this collection of his views will provide an interesting sidelight on his books. For aspiring writers who are looking for practical advice on the demanding task of putting words together, these pages will be a gold mine of observations, suggestions, and tricks of the trade.

As Hemingway's publisher and friend, I think it would have pleased him to know that some of the things he learned about literary creation were being shared with writers of another generation. I'm sure he would have come out with some wry or disparaging remark about his own work, but down deep I think he would have been grateful to Larry Phillips for collecting his views on writing in this useful and interesting way.

Charles Scribner, Jr.

Preface

THROUGHOUT Ernest Hemingway's career as a writer, he maintained that it was bad luck to talk about writing—that it takes off "whatever butterflies have on their wings and the arrangement of hawk's feathers if you show it or talk about it."

Despite this belief, by the end of his life he had done just what he intended not to do. In his novels and stories, in letters to editors, friends, fellow artists, and critics, in interviews and in commissioned articles on the subject, Hemingway wrote often about writing. And he wrote as well and as incisively about the subject as any writer who ever lived. His comments and observations on the craft accumulated over his lifetime into a substantial body of work—comments which are, for the

most part, easy to excerpt from the text surrounding
them.

The process which led to this collection began
several years ago, and had its start, as perhaps all such
books have their start, with my admiration for the author
and his writing, and with my own search for the rules of
writing. The idea was originally inspired by Thomas H.
Moore, who did a similar book on Henry Miller, noting
as he went passages which touched on the subject of
writing, and collecting them.

Collecting the opinions of one man on a given subject, as expressed throughout a lifetime, proved to be an
interesting exercise. As with anyone's thoughts on a
given subject, Hemingway's on writing were scattered,
so to speak, to the four corners of his world. As I brought
them together again, and assembled them into different
categories, something unusual happened. Comments ap-
parently made at random, at different times, often decades
apart, and in different cities or countries, magically began
to fit together like pieces of a puzzle.

This is perhaps similar to the effect known to tran-
scribers of taped interviews in which a person will sometimes leave a subject in mid-sentence, go on to talk about
something else for a time, then resume again the original
thought, taking up at the precise point where he left off.
When Hemingway's isolated comments on the subject
of writing were taken out of widely diverse articles,

letters, and books, they locked together like some message issued over the years, dictated between the lines of other material. I have attempted here to preserve some of that feeling.

This book contains Hemingway's reflections on the nature of the writer and on elements of the writer's life, including specific and helpful advice to writers on the craft of writing, work habits, and discipline. The Hemingway personality comes through in general wisdom, wit, humor, and insight, and in his insistence on the integrity of the writer and of the profession itself.

I hope that this book will be an aid and inspiration to writers everywhere, for students of writing, and for the general reader—to have collected here in one volume what otherwise would have to be looked up or searched for. Some writers, as Hemingway said in *Green Hills of Africa*, are born only to help another writer to write one sentence. I hope this collection will contribute to the making of many sentences.

Grateful acknowledgment is due to Charles Scribner, Jr., and Michael Pietsch of Charles Scribner's Sons for their invaluable assistance in the preparation of this book.

Monroe, Wisconsin   LARRY W. PHILLIPS
January 1984

ERNEST HEMINGWAY
ON WRITING

ONE

What Writing Is
and Does

⤚⤙

I AM trying to make, before I get through, a
picture of the whole world—or as much of it as I have
seen. Boiling it down always, rather than spreading it
out thin.

to Mrs. Paul Pfeiffer, 1933
Selected Letters, p. 397

⌒

All good books are alike in that they are truer than
if they had really happened and after you are finished
reading one you will feel that all that happened to you
and afterwards it all belongs to you; the good and the

[3]

bad, the ecstasy, the remorse and sorrow, the people and the places and how the weather was.

By-Line: Ernest Hemingway, p. 184

~

"Nobody really knows or understands and nobody has ever said the secret. The secret is that it is poetry written into prose and it is the hardest of all things to do . . ."

from MARY HEMINGWAY, *How It Was, p. 352*

~

Then there is the other secret. There isn't any symbolysm (mis-spelled). The sea is the sea. The old man is an old man. The boy is a boy and the fish is a fish. The shark are all sharks no better and no worse. All the symbolism that people say is shit. What goes beyond is what you see beyond when you know.

to Bernard Berenson, 1952
Selected Letters, p. 780

~

In truly good writing no matter how many times you read it you do not know how it is done. That is because there is a mystery in all great writing and that mystery does not dis-sect out. It continues and it is always valid. Each time you re-read you see or learn something new.

to Harvey Breit, 1952
Selected Letters, p. 770

◇

When you first start writing stories in the first person if the stories are made so real that people believe them the people reading them nearly always think the stories really happened to you. That is natural because while you were making them up you had to make them happen to the person who was telling them. If you do this successfully enough you make the person who is reading them believe that the things happened to him too. If you can do this you are beginning to get what you are trying for which is to make the story so real beyond any reality that it will become a part of the reader's experience and a part of his memory. There must be things that he did not notice when he read the story or the novel which without his knowing it, enter into his

[5]

memory and experience so that they are a part of his life. This is not easy to do.

unpublished manuscript
from the Kennedy Library
collection, Roll 19, T 178

∽

It's enough for you to do it once for a few men to remember you. But if you do it year after year, then many people remember you and they tell it to their children, and their children and grandchildren remember and, if it concerns books, they can read them. And if it's good enough, it will last as long as there are human beings.

from MALCOLM COWLEY, *"A Portrait of Mr. Papa"*
Life Jan. 10, 1949

The Qualities of a Writer

ALL my life I've looked at words as though I were seeing them for the first time . . .

to Mary Welsh, 1945
Selected Letters, p. 583

First, there must be talent, much talent. Talent such as Kipling had. Then there must be discipline. The discipline of Flaubert. Then there must be the conception of what it can be and an absolute conscience as unchanging as the standard meter in Paris, to prevent faking. Then the writer must be intelligent and disinterested and above all he must survive. Try to get all these in one person and have him come through all the influences that press on a writer. The hardest thing, because time is so short, is for him to survive and get his work done.

Green Hills of Africa, p. 27

❧

. . . real seriousness in regard to writing being one of the two absolute necessities. The other, unfortunately, is talent.

By-Line: Ernest Hemingway, p. 214

❧

The most essential gift for a good writer is a built-in, shockproof, shit detector. This is the writer's radar and all great writers have had it.

from GEORGE PLIMPTON,
"An Interview with Ernest Hemingway"
The Paris Review 18, Spring 1958

❧

A writer without a sense of justice and of injustice would be better off editing the year book of a school for exceptional children than writing novels.

from GEORGE PLIMPTON,
"An Interview with Ernest Hemingway"
The Paris Review 18, Spring 1958

A good writer should know as near everything as possible. Naturally he will not. A great enough writer seems to be born with knowledge. But he really is not; he has only been born with the ability to learn in a quicker ratio to the passage of time than other men and without conscious application, and with an intelligence to accept or reject what is already presented as knowledge. There are some things which cannot be learned quickly and time, which is all we have, must be paid heavily for their acquiring. They are the very simplest things and because it takes a man's life to know them the little new that each man gets from life is very costly and the only heritage he has to leave. Every novel which is truly written contributes to the total knowledge which is there at the disposal of the next writer who comes, but the next writer must pay, always, a certain nominal percentage in experience to be able to understand and assimilate what is available as his birthright and what he must, in turn, take his departure from.

Death in the Afternoon, pp. 191–192

~

Good writing is true writing. If a man is making a story up it will be true in proportion to the amount of knowledge of life that he has and how conscientious he is; so that when he makes something up it is as it would truly be.

By-Line: Ernest Hemingway, p. 215

~

Mice: Then what about imagination?

Y.C.: It is the one thing beside honesty that a good writer must have. The more he learns from experience the more truly he can imagine. If he gets so he can imagine truly enough people will think that the things he relates all really happened and that he is just reporting.

By-Line: Ernest Hemingway, p. 215

{Editor's note: Hemingway, writing as "Your Correspondent," abbreviated the words to "Y.C." "Mice" is the nickname by which Y.C. addresses a young writer.}

Mice: What is the best early training for a writer?
Y.C.: An unhappy childhood.

By-Line: Ernest Hemingway, p. 219

THREE

The Pain and Pleasure
of Writing

INTERVIEWER: Can you recall an exact moment
when you decided to become a writer?
HEMINGWAY: No, I always wanted to be a writer.
from GEORGE PLIMPTON,
"An Interview with Ernest Hemingway"
The Paris Review 18, Spring 1958

I believe that basically you write for two people;
yourself to try to make it absolutely perfect; or if not
that then wonderful. Then you write for who you love

whether she can read or write or not and whether she is
alive or dead.

to Arthur Mizener, 1950
Selected Letters, p. 694

❦

Will work again on the novel today. Writing is a
hard business Max but nothing makes you feel better.

to Maxwell Perkins, 1938
Selected Letters, p. 474

❦

Been working every day and going good. Makes a
hell of a dull life too. But it is more fun than anything
else. Do you remember how old [Ford Madox] Ford was
always writing how [Joseph] Conrad suffered so when
he wrote? How it was un metier du chien {a dog's trade}
etc. Do you suffer when you write? I don't at all. Suffer
like a bastard when don't write, or just before, and feel
empty and fucked out afterwards. But never feel as good
as while writing.

to Malcolm Cowley, 1945
Selected Letters, pp. 604–605

❧

. . . writing is something that you can never do as well as it can be done. It is a perpetual challenge and it is more difficult than anything else that I have ever done— so I do it. And it makes me happy when I do it well.

to Ivan Kashkin, 1935
Selected Letters, p. 419

❧

Am here in La Coruna waiting for proof. . . . Which now ought to be here and I hope to God it comes. Need to read some bloody thing I've written in order to convince myself that ever have written anything in order to eventually write something else. Maybe you know the feeling.

to Barklie McKee Henry, 1927
Selected Letters, p. 254

❧

Charlie there is no future in anything. I hope you agree. That is why I like it at a war. Every day and

[15]

every night there is a strong possibility that you will get killed and not have to write. I have to write to be happy whether I get paid for it or not. But it is a hell of a disease to be born with. I like to do it. Which is even worse. That makes it from a disease into a vice. Then I want to do it better than anybody has ever done it which makes it into an obsession. An obsession is terrible. Hope you haven't gotten any. That's the only one I've got left.

to Charles Scribner, 1940
Selected Letters, pp. 503–504

You know that fiction, prose rather, is possibly the roughest trade of all in writing. You do not have the reference, the old important reference. You have the sheet of blank paper, the pencil, and the obligation to invent truer than things can be true. You have to take what is not palpable and make it completely palpable and also have it seem normal and so that it can become a part of the experience of the person who reads it.

to Bernard Berenson, 1954
Selected Letters, p. 837

"Do you think your writing is worth doing—as an end in itself?"

"Oh, yes."

"You are sure?"

"Very sure."

"That must be very pleasant."

"It is," I said. "It is the one altogether pleasant thing about it."

Green Hills of Africa, p. 26

～

He always worked best when Helen was unwell. Just that much discontent and friction. Then there were times when you had to write. Not conscience. Just peristaltic action. Then you felt sometimes like you could never write but after a while you knew sooner or later you would write another good story.

It was really more fun than anything. That was really why you did it. He had never realized that before. It wasn't conscience. It was simply that it was the greatest pleasure. It had more bite to it than anything else.

The Nick Adams Stories, p. 238

～

There's no rule on how it is to write. Sometimes it comes easily and perfectly. Sometimes it is like drilling rock and then blasting it out with charges.

to Charles Poore, 1953
Selected Letters, pp. 800–801

◡

I love to write. But it has never gotten any easier to do and you can't expect it to if you keep trying for something better than you can do.

to L. H. Brague, Jr., 1959
Selected Letters, p. 893

FOUR

What to Write About

⟶

THE good parts of a book may be only something
a writer is lucky enough to overhear or it may be the
wreck of his whole damn life—and one is as good as the
other.

to F. Scott Fitzgerald, 1929
Selected Letters, p. 305

⌒

Forget your personal tragedy. We are all bitched
from the start and you especially have to be hurt like
hell before you can write seriously. But when you get the
damned hurt use it—don't cheat with it. Be as faithful

[19]

to it as a scientist—but don't think anything is of any importance because it happens to you or anyone belonging to you.

> to F. Scott Fitzgerald, 1934
> *Selected Letters, p. 408*

◇

A man's got to take a lot of punishment to write a really funny book.

> to William B. Smith, Jr., 1924
> *Selected Letters, p. 139*

◇

Dostoevsky was made by being sent to Siberia. Writers are forged in injustice as a sword is forged.

> *Green Hills of Africa, p. 71*

◇

So the boys can't tell a story. You know why? They couldn't tell it if they put them on the stand. If you have a story it is not hard to tell. Maybe people won't believe it. But you can tell it straight and true.

A writer, of course, has to make up stories for them to be rounded and not flat like photographs. But he makes them up out of what he knows.

to Charles Scribner, 1949
Selected Letters, p. 678

❧

. . . whatever success I have had has been through writing what I know about.

to Maxwell Perkins, 1928
Selected Letters, p. 273

❧

Up in that room I decided that I would write one story about each thing that I knew about. I was trying to do this all the time I was writing, and it was good and severe discipline.

A Moveable Feast, p. 12

❧

... I figure it is better to write about what you can write about and try and make it come off than have epoch making canvasses etc.—and you figure what age the novelists had that wrote the really great novels.

to Maxwell Perkins, 1926
Selected Letters, pp. 229–230

❧

The one thing that I will not do is repeat myself on anything so the new ones are rarely as popular—people always want a story like the last one.

to Maxwell Perkins, 1932
Selected Letters, p. 377

❧

I wish I could write well enough to write about air-craft. Faulkner did it very well in Pylon but you cannot do something some one else has done though you might have done it if they hadn't.

to Harvey Breit, 1956
Selected Letters, p. 863

❧

. . . I thought about Tolstoi and about what a great advantage an experience of war was to a writer. It was one of the major subjects and certainly one of the hardest to write truly of and those writers who had not seen it were always very jealous and tried to make it seem unimportant, or abnormal, or a disease as a subject, while, really, it was just something quite irreplaceable that they had missed.

Green Hills of Africa, p. 70

╭◦

For your information in stories about the war I try to show *all* the different sides of it, taking it slowly and honestly and examining it from many ways. So never think one story represents my viewpoint because it is much too complicated for that.

We know war is bad. Yet sometimes it is necessary to fight. But still war is bad and any man who says it is not is a liar. But it is very complicated and difficult to write about truly. For instance to take it on a simply personal basis—in the war in Italy when I was a boy I had much fear. In Spain I had no fear after a couple of weeks and was very happy. Yet for me to not understand fear in others or deny its existence would be bad writing.

[23]

It is just that now I understand the whole thing better. . . .

I would like to be able to write understandingly about both deserters and heroes, cowards and brave men, traitors and men who are not capable of being traitors. We learned a lot about all such people.

to Russian critic Ivan Kashkin, 1939
Selected Letters, p. 480

∽

. . . civil war is the best war for a writer, the most complete. Stendhal had seen a war and Napoleon taught him to write. He was teaching everybody then; but no one else learned.

Green Hills of Africa, p. 71

∽

Like me to write you a little essay on The Importance of Subject? Well the reason you are so sore you missed the war is because war is the best subject of all. It groups the maximum of material and speeds up the action and brings out all sorts of stuff that normally

[24]

you have to wait a lifetime to get. What made 3 Soldiers
a swell book was the war. What made Streets of Night
a lousy book was Boston. . . . One was as well written
as the other, I can hear you telling me I'm all wrong.
Maybe I am. Love is also a good subject as you might be
said to have discovered. Other major subjects are the
money from which we get riches and poores. Also
avarice. Gentlemen the boy lecturer is tired. A dull
subject I should say would be impotence. Murder is a
good one so get a swell murder into yr. next book and
sit back.

> to F. Scott Fitzgerald, 1925
> *Selected Letters, pp. 176–177*

Such damned exciting things happen in our own
time that it is hard to leave Now, if you have seen the
things, to go back into a fictional past unless they project
it very wonderfully.

> to Charles Scribner, 1947
> *Selected Letters, p. 631*

The hardest thing in the world to do is to write straight honest prose on human beings. First you have to know the subject; then you have to know how to write. Both take a lifetime to learn . . .

By-Line: Ernest Hemingway, p. 183

⌣

Madame, all stories, if continued far enough, end in death, and he is no true-story teller who would keep that from you.

Death in the Afternoon, p. 122

FIVE

Advice to Writers

~

I WAS trying to learn to write, commencing with
the simplest things . . .

Death in the Afternoon, p. 2

~

Look how it is at the start—all juice and kick to
the writer and cant convey anything to the reader—you
use up the juice and the kick goes but you learn how to
do it and the stuff when you are no longer young is
better than the young stuff—

to F. Scott Fitzgerald, 1929
Selected Letters, p. 306

[27]

⌒

... sometimes when I was starting a new story and I could not get it going, I would sit in front of the fire and squeeze the peel of the little oranges into the edge of the flame and watch the sputter of blue that they made. I would stand and look out over the roofs of Paris and think, "Do not worry. You have always written before and you will write now. All you have to do is write one true sentence. Write the truest sentence that you know." So finally I would write one true sentence, and then go on from there. It was easy then because there was always one true sentence that I knew or had seen or had heard someone say. If I started to write elaborately, or like someone introducing or presenting something, I found that I could cut that scrollwork or ornament out and throw it away and start with the first true simple declarative sentence I had written.

A Moveable Feast, p. 12

⌒

I was trying to write then and I found the greatest difficulty, aside from knowing truly what you really felt,

rather than what you were supposed to feel, and had
been taught to feel, was to put down what really
happened in action; what the actual things were which
produced the emotion that you experienced. In writing
for a newspaper you told what happened and, with one
trick and another, you communicated the emotion
aided by the element of timeliness which gives a certain
emotion to any account of something that has happened
on that day; but the real thing, the sequence of motion
and fact which made the emotion and which would be as
valid in a year or in ten years or, with luck and if you
stated it purely enough, always, was beyond me and I
was working very hard to get it.

Death in the Afternoon, p. 2

For myself . . . the problem was one of depiction
and waking in the night I tried to remember what it was
that seemed just out of my remembering and that was
the thing that I had really seen and, finally, remembering
all around it, I got it. When he [matador] stood up, his
face white and dirty and the silk of his breeches opened
from waist to knee, it was the dirtiness of the rented
breeches, the dirtiness of his slit underwear and the clean,

clean, unbearably clean whiteness of the thigh bone
that I had seen, and it was that which was important.

Death in the Afternoon, p. 20

⌒

Mice: How can a writer train himself?

Y.C.: Watch what happens today. If we get into a
fish see exactly what it is that everyone does. If you get
a kick out of it while he is jumping remember back
until you see exactly what the action was that gave you
the emotion. Whether it was the rising of the line from
the water and the way it tightened like a fiddle string
until drops started from it, or the way he smashed and
threw water when he jumped. Remember what the
noises were and what was said. Find what gave you the
emotion; what the action was that gave you the
excitement. Then write it down making it clear so the
reader will see it too and have the same feeling that you
had. That's a five finger exercise.

Mice: All right.

Y.C.: Then get in somebody else's head for a
change. If I bawl you out try to figure what I'm thinking
about as well as how you feel about it. If Carlos curses
Juan think what both their sides of it are. Don't just

think who is right. As a man things are as they should or
shouldn't be. As a man you know who is right and who
is wrong. You have to make decisions and enforce them.
As a writer you should not judge. You should understand.

Mice: All right.

Y.C.: Listen *now*. When people talk listen
completely. Don't be thinking what you're going to say.
Most people never listen. Nor do they observe. You
should be able to go into a room and when you come
out know everything that you saw there and not only
that. If that room gave you any feeling you should know
exactly what it was that gave you that feeling. Try that
for practice. When you're in town stand outside the
theatre and see how the people differ in the way they get
out of taxis or motor cars. There are a thousands ways
to practice. And always think of other people.

By-Line: Ernest Hemingway, pp. 219–20

～

Second place, a long time ago you stopped listening
except to the answers to your own questions. You had
good stuff in too that it didn't need. That's what dries a
writer up (we all dry up. That's no insult to you in
person) not listening. That is where it all comes from.

Seeing, listening. You see well enough. But you stop listening.

to F. Scott Fitzgerald, 1934
Selected Letters, p. 407

༄

. . . Pamplona is changed, of course, but not as much as we are older. . . . We've seen it all go and we'll watch it go again. The great thing is to last and get your work done and see and hear and learn and understand; and write when there is something that you know; and not before; and not too damned much after. Let those who want to save the world if you can get to see it clear and as a whole. Then any part you make will represent the whole if it's made truly. The thing to do is work and learn to make it.

Death in the Afternoon, p. 278

༄

.". . . I'm trying to do it so it will make it without you knowing it, and so the more you read it, the more there will be."

A Moveable Feast, p. 138

❧

You see I'm trying in all my stories to get the feeling of the actual life across—not to just depict life—or criticize it—but to actually make it alive. So that when you have read something by me you actually experience the thing. You can't do this without putting in the bad and the ugly as well as what is beautiful. Because if it is all beautiful you can't believe in it. Things aren't that way. It is only by showing both sides—3 dimensions and if possible 4 that you can write the way I want to.

to Dr. C. E. Hemingway, 1925
Selected Letters, p. 153

❧

Since I had started to break down all my writing and get rid of all facility and try to make instead of describe, writing had been wonderful to do. But it was very difficult, and I did not know how I would ever write anything as long as a novel. It often took me a full morning of work to write a paragraph.

A Moveable Feast, p. 156

⌁

I try always to do the thing by three cushion shots rather than by words or direct statement. But maybe we must have the direct statement too.

to Owen Wister, 1929
Selected Letters, p. 301

⌁

This is the prose that I have been working for all my life [*The Old Man and the Sea*] that should read easily and simply and seem short and yet have all the dimensions of the visible world and the world of a man's spirit. It is as good prose as I can write as of now.

to Charles Scribner, 1951
Selected Letters, p. 738

⌁

[Ezra was] . . . the man who had taught me to distrust adjectives as I would later learn to distrust certain people in certain situations . . .

A Moveable Feast, p. 134

[34]

≺

". . . Your first seeing of a country is a very
valuable one. Probably more valuable to yourself than
to any one else, is the hell of it. But you ought to always
write it to try to get it stated. No matter what you do
with it."

Green Hills of Africa, p. 193

≺

I like to have Gertrude [Stein] bawl me out because
it keeps one['s] opinion of oneself down—way down—
She liked the book very much she said—But what I
wanted to hear about was what she didnt like and why·—
She thinks the parts that fail are where I remember
visually rather than make up . . .

to F. Scott Fitzgerald, 1929
Selected Letters, p. 310

≺

. . . I went to Spain . . . where I'm trying to do the
country like Cezanne and having a hell of a time and

sometimes getting it a little bit. . . . It is about 100 pages
long and nothing happens and the country is swell, I
made it all up, so I see it all and part of it comes out the
way it ought to . . .

to Gertrude Stein, 1924
Selected Letters, p. 122

⌒

What I've been doing is trying to do country so you
don't remember the words after you read it but actually
have the Country. It is hard because to do it you have
to see the country all complete all the time you write
and not just have a romantic feeling about it.

to Edward O'Brien, 1924
Selected Letters, p. 123

⌒

Some days it went so well that you could make the
country so that you could walk into it through the timber
to come out into the clearing and work up onto the
high ground and see the hills beyond the arm of the lake.

A Moveable Feast, p. 91

He wanted to write like Cezanne painted.

Cezanne started with all the tricks. Then he broke the whole thing down and built the real thing. It was hell to do. He was the greatest. The greatest for always. It wasn't a cult. He, Nick, wanted to write about country so it would be there like Cezanne had done it in painting. You had to do it from inside yourself. There wasn't any trick. Nobody had ever written about country like that. He felt almost holy about it. It was deadly serious. You could do it if you would fight it out. If you'd lived right with your eyes.

The Nick Adams Stories, p. 239

Remember to get the weather in your god damned book—weather is very important.

to John Dos Passos, 1932
Selected Letters, p. 355

My attitude toward punctuation is that it ought to be as conventional as *possible*. The game of golf would lose a good deal if croquet mallets and billiard cues were allowed on the putting green. You ought to be

[37]

able to show that you can do it a good deal better than anyone else with the regular tools before you have a license to bring in your own improvements.

to Horace Liveright, 1925
Selected Letters, p. 161

⌒

Actually if a writer needs a dictionary he should not write. He should have read the dictionary at least three times from beginning to end and then have loaned it to someone who needs it. There are only certain words which are valid and similies (bring me my dictionary) are like defective ammunition (the lowest thing I can think of at this time).

to Bernard Berenson, 1953
Selected Letters, p. 809

⌒

INTERVIEWER: Would you suggest newspaper work for the young writer? How helpful was the training you had with the *Kansas City Star?*

HEMINGWAY: On the *Star* you were forced to learn to write a simple declarative sentence. This is useful to

[38]

anyone. Newspaper work will not harm a young writer
and could help him if he gets out of it in time.

from GEORGE PLIMPTON,
"An Interview with Ernest Hemingway"
The Paris Review 18, Spring 1958

Have been work very hard on this book. She pretty
near over. All that remains now is to perform the
unperformable miracle you have to always do at the end.

to Archibald MacLeish, 1936
Selected Letters, p. 453

After a book I am emotionally exhausted. If you
are not you have not transferred the emotion completely
to the reader. Anyway that is the way it works with me.

to Charles Scribner, Jr., 1952
Selected Letters, p. 778

SIX

Working Habits

Mice: Do you know what is going to happen when you write a story?

Y.C.: Almost never. I start to make it up and have happen what would have to happen as it goes along.

By-Line: Ernest Hemingway, p. 217

❧

Mice: How much should you write a day?

Y.C.: The best way is always to stop when you are going good and when you know what will happen next. If you do that every day when you are writing a novel you will never be stuck. That is the most valuable thing I can tell you so try to remember it.

Mice: All right.

Y.C.: Always stop while you are going good and don't think about it or worry about it until you start to write the next day. That way your subconscious will work on it all the time. But if you think about it consciously or worry about it you will kill it and your brain will be tired before you start. Once you are into the novel it is as cowardly to worry about whether you can go on the next day as to worry about having to go into inevitable action. You *have* to go on. So there is no sense to worry. You have to learn that to write a novel. The hard part about a novel is to finish it.

Mice: How can you learn not to worry?

Y.C.: By not thinking about it. As soon as you start to think about it stop it. Think about something else. You have to learn that.

By-Line: Ernest Hemingway, pp. 216–217

⌒

When I was writing, it was necessary for me to read after I had written. If you kept thinking about it, you would lose the thing that you were writing before you could go on with it the next day. It was necessary to get exercise, to be tired in the body, and it was very good to make love with whom you loved. That was better than anything. But afterwards, when you were empty, it was necessary to read in order not to think or worry about your work until you could do it again. I had learned already never to empty the well of my writing, but always to stop when there was still something there in the deep part of the well, and let it refill at night from the springs that fed it.

To keep my mind off writing sometimes after I had worked I would read writers who were writing then, such as Aldous Huxley, D. H. Lawrence or any who had books published that I could get from Sylvia Beach's library or find along the quais.

A Moveable Feast, pp. 25–26

⌒

It was in that room too that I learned not to think about anything that I was writing from the time I stopped writing until I started again the next day. That way my subconscious would be working on it and at the same time I would be listening to other people and noticing everything, I hoped; learning, I hoped; and I would read so that I would not think about my work and make myself impotent to do it. Going down the stairs when I had worked well, and that needed luck as well as discipline, was a wonderful feeling and I was free then to walk anywhere in Paris.

A Moveable Feast, p. 13

❧

After writing a story I was always empty and both sad and happy, as though I had made love, and I was sure this was a very good story although I would not know truly how good until I read it over the next day.

A Moveable Feast, p. 6

❧

Mice: How much do you read over every day before you start to write?

Y.C.: The best way is to read it all every day from the start, correcting as you go along, then go on from where you stopped the day before. When it gets so long that you can't do this every day read back two or three chapters each day; then each week read it all from the start. That's how you make it all of one piece. And remember to stop while you are still going good. That keeps it moving instead of having it die whenever you go on and write yourself out. When you do that you find that the next day you are pooped and can't go on.

By-Line: Ernest Hemingway, p. 217

～

Scott took LITERATURE so solemnly. He never understood that it was just writing as well as you can and finishing what you start.

to Arthur Mizener, 1950
Selected Letters, p. 695

～

You just have to *go on* when it is worst and most helpless—there is only one thing to do with a novel and that is go straight on through to the end of the damn thing.

to F. Scott Fitzgerald, 1929
Selected Letters, p. 306

～

[45]

Would like to finish this [*A Farewell to Arms*] down here if possible, put it away for a couple or three months and then re-write it. The re-writing doesn't take more than six weeks or two months once it is done. But it is pretty important for me to let it cool off well before re-writing.

to Maxwell Perkins, 1928
Selected Letters, pp. 276–277

❧

Let me know how long I have to stay away from it before I can get it to you. Longer I can stay away before I have to get it to you the better it will be as gives me a whole new chance to see it cold and plug any gaps and amplify where there is any need.

to Charles Scribner, 1949
Selected Letters, p. 684

❧

Coming back here I am anxious to start re-writing the book [*A Farewell to Arms*]. But it is only a month since I finished it and it probably is best to let it lie until we get settled in Florida. I finished the Sun in

Sept. and did not start re-writing it until December. This
will not take as much re-writing as each day to start
with (while I was working on it) I wrote over what I
had done the day before. But I want to make sure that I
leave it alone long enough so I can find the places where
I get the kick when writing it and neglect to convey it
to the reader.

to Maxwell Perkins, 1928
Selected Letters, p. 285

Ordinarily I never read anything before I write in
the morning to try and bite on the old nail with no help,
no influence and no one giving you a wonderful example
or sitting looking over your shoulder.

to Bernard Berenson, 1952
Selected Letters, p. 790

The blue-backed notebooks, the two pencils and
the pencil sharpener (a pocket knife was too wasteful),
the marble-topped tables, the smell of early morning,
sweeping out and mopping, were all you needed. For
luck you carried a horse chestnut and a rabbit's foot in

your right pocket. The fur had been worn off the rabbit's foot long ago and the bones and the sinews were polished by wear. The claws scratched in the lining of your pocket and you knew your luck was still there.

A Moveable Feast, p. 91

❧

So I am going to write on on that [*For Whom the Bell Tolls*] until it is finished. I wish I could show it to you so far because I am very proud of it but that is bad luck too. So is talking about it.

to Maxwell Perkins, 1939
Selected Letters, p. 482

❧

However am now going to write a swell novel—will not talk about it on acct. the greater ease of talking about it than writing it and consequent danger of doing same.

to F. Scott Fitzgerald, 1927
Selected Letters, p. 261

❧

Two weeks ago let Miss Mary read what had been
writing on acct. never let anybody read it on acct. it takes
off whatever butterflies have on their wings and the
arrangement of hawk's feathers if you show it or talk
about it. But thought . . . ought to show her whether was
just jerking off in the tower or trying to hit the ball
sharp and solid without trying to pull it for the owners.

to Lillian Ross, 1948
Selected Letters, p. 649

⌒

Under the charm of these rich I was as trusting and
as stupid as a bird dog who wants to go out with any
man with a gun, or a trained pig in a circus who has
finally found someone who loves and appreciates him for
himself alone. That every day should be a fiesta seemed
to me a marvelous discovery. I even read aloud the part
of the novel that I had rewritten, which is about as low
as a writer can get and much more dangerous for him
as a writer than glacier skiing unroped before the full
winter snowfall has set over the crevices.

When they said, "It's great, Ernest. Truly it's great.
You cannot know the thing it has," I wagged my tail
in pleasure and plunged into the fiesta concept of life
to see if I could not bring some fine attractive stick back,

instead of thinking, "If these bastards like it what is wrong with it?" That was what I would think if I had been functioning as a professional although, if I had been functioning as a professional, I would never have read it to them.

A Moveable Feast, p. 209

＞

You see it's awfully hard to talk or write about your own stuff because if it is any good you yourself know about how good it is—but if you say so yourself you feel like a shit.

to Malcolm Cowley, 1945
Selected Letters, p. 603

＞

He started to talk about my writing and I stopped listening. It made me feel sick for people to talk about my writing to my face . . .

A Moveable Feast, p. 127

＞

[50]

Writing and travel broaden your ass if not your
mind and I like to write standing up.

> to Harvey Breit, 1950
> *Selected Letters, p.* 700

◇

When you start to write you get all the kick and
the reader gets none. So you might as well use a
typewriter because it is that much easier and you enjoy
it that much more. After you learn to write your whole
object is to convey everything, every sensation, sight,
feeling, place and emotion to the reader. To do this you
have to work over what you write. If you write with a
pencil you get three different sights at it to see if the
reader is getting what you want him to. First when you
read it over; then when it is typed you get another
chance to improve it, and again in the proof. Writing it
first in pencil gives you one-third more chance to
improve it. That is .333 which is a damned good average
for a hitter. It also keeps it fluid longer so that you can
better it easier.

> *By-Line: Ernest Hemingway, p.* 216

◇

Am in sort of a better epoque of working now and just remembered that I always work well in the Spring.

to Arnold Gingrich, 1936
Selected Letters, p. 441

❧

No one can work every day in the hot months without going stale. To break up the pattern of work, we fish the Gulf Stream in the spring and summer months and in the fall.

By-Line: Ernest Hemingway, p. 472

❧

That terrible mood of depression of whether it's any good or not is what is known as The Artist's Reward. . . .

Summer's a discouraging time to work—You dont feel death coming on the way it does in the fall when the boys really put pen to paper.

Everybody loses all the bloom—we're not peaches —that doesnt mean you get rotten—a gun is better worn and with bloom off—So is a saddle—People too by

God. You lose everything that is fresh and everything that is easy and it always seems as though you could *never* write—But you have more metier and you know more and when you get flashes of the old juice you get more results with them.

> to F. Scott Fitzgerald, 1929
> *Selected Letters, p. 306*

￮

Have never known a summer to go so fast. When am working as hard as have been since the first week in April the days all just blur together. . . . Wake about seven thirty, have breakfast and am working by nine and usually work straight through until two p.m. After that it's like living in a vacuum until working time next day.

> to Mrs. Paul Pfeiffer, 1939
> *Selected Letters, p. 491*

￮

It was a pleasant café, warm and clean and friendly, and I hung up my old waterproof on the coat rack to dry and put my worn and weathered felt hat on the

rack above the bench and ordered a *café au lait*. The
waiter brought it and I took out a notebook from the
pocket of the coat and a pencil and started to write. I
was writing about up in Michigan and since it was a
wild, cold, blowing day it was that sort of day in the
story.

A Moveable Feast, p. 5

◇

There's only 6 weeks more of bad weather to get
through and then we will have the type of weather that
makes you want to write rather than force yourself to
write. I am such a simple writer that in my books the
temperature and the weather of the day is nearly almost
that of the weather outside. The type of weather we
have had this summer I would not wish to inflict on
anyone reading what I write and so I'm working in an
air-conditioned room which is as false a way to work as to
try to write in the pressurized cabin of a plane. You get
the writing done but it's as false as though it were done
in the reverse of a greenhouse. Probably I will throw it
all away, but maybe when the mornings are alive again
I can use the skeleton of what I have written and fill it in
with the smells and the early noises of the birds and all

[54]

the lovely things of this finca which are in the cold
months very much like Africa.

to Bernard Berenson, 1954
Selected Letters, p. 838

❧

Eased off on the book . . . in May because Dr. said I
worked too hard in April, and May fine month to fish
and make love to Miss Mary. I have to ease off on
makeing love when writing hard as the two things are
run by the same motor.

to Charles Scribner, 1948
Selected Letters, p. 636

❧

Having books published is very destructive to
writing. It is even worse than making love too much.
Because when you make love too much at least you get a
damned clarte that is like no other light. A very clear
and hollow light.

to Bernard Berenson, 1952
Selected Letters, p. 785

The more I'm let alone and not worried the better
I can function.

> to Grace Hall Hemingway, 1929
> *Selected Letters, p. 296*

I loved to write very much and was never happier
than doing it. Charlie's [Scribner's] ridiculing of my
daily word count was because he did not understand me
or writing especially well nor could know how happy
one felt to have put down properly 422 words as you
wanted them to be. And days of 1200 or 2700 were
something that made you happier than you could believe.
Since I found that 400 to 600 well done was a pace I
could hold much better was always happy with that
number. But if I only had 320 I felt good.

> to Maxwell Perkins, 1944
> *Selected Letters, p. 557*

Don't worry about the words. I've been doing that since 1921. I always count them when I knock off and am drinking the first whiskey and soda. Guess I got in the habit writing dispatches. Used to send them from some places where they cost a dollar and a quarter a word and you had to make them awful interesting at that price or get fired.

to Charles Scribner, 1940
Selected Letters, p. 503

Am writing large and clear if you can read it then it is a help to me because I hate the typewriter (my new one) and I must not write letters on any old one because it has page 594 of the [African] book in it, covered over with the dust cover, and it is unlucky to take the pages out.

to Bernard Berenson, 1955
Selected Letters, p. 847

. . . to write I go back to the old desolation of a hotel bed room I started to write in. Tell everybody you

live in one hotel and live in another. When they locate
you in the other move to the country. When they
locate you in the country move somewhere else. Work
everyday till your so pooped about all the exercise you
can face is reading the papers. Then eat, play tennis or
swim or something in a work daze just to keep your
bowells moveing and the next day write again.

to Thomas Shevlin, 1939
Selected Letters, p. 484

◇

Am very ashamed not to have written. Was
over-run by journalists, photographers and plain and
fancy crazies. Was in the middle of writing a book and it
is a little like being interrupted in fornication.

to Gen. E. E. Dorman-O'Gowan, 1954
Selected Letters, p. 843

◇

The present situation here would offer a wonderful
opportunity for a man with real directorial ability to
show how creative writing could be done at the same
time as running a carry them by hand elevator service,

and superintend plumbers, the re-doing of a leaking roof, wiring of house, installation of water system, carpenters etc. while trying to keep someone under doctors orders not to walk upstairs from walking upstairs etc. A wonderful directorial job wasted on someone that doesn't appreciate it. The minute I quit trying to write the rest of it is easy.

to Mrs. Paul Pfeiffer, 1932
Selected Letters, p. 348

◇

I happen to be in a very tough business where there are no alibis. It is good or it is bad and the thousand reasons that interfere with a book being as good as possible are no excuses if it is not. You have to make it good and a man is a fool if he adds or takes hindrance after hindrance after hindrance to being a writer when that is what he cares about. Taking refuge in domestic successes, being good to your broke friends etc. is merely a form of quitting.

to Mrs. Paul Pfeiffer, 1932
Selected Letters, p. 350

◇

Well all of that is why I haven't written you. There have been other interruptions of all sorts but I am fairly ruthless about them. Have a big sign on the gate that says in Spanish Mr. H. receives no one without a previous appointment. Save yourself the annoyance of not being received by not comeing to the house. Then if they do come up I have a right to curse them off.

to Maxwell Perkins, 1947
Selected Letters, pp. 616–617

∾

To discourage visitors while he is at work your correspondent has hired an aged negro who appears to be the victim of an odd disease resembling leprosy who meets visitors at the gate and says, "I'se Mr. Hemingway and I'se crazy about you."

By-Line: Ernest Hemingway, p. 192

∾

Since the good old days when Charles Baudelaire led a purple lobster on a leash through the same old Latin Quarter, there has not been much good poetry written in cafes. Even then I suspect that Baudelaire

parked the lobster with the concierge down on the first
floor, put the chloroform bottle corked on the washstand
and sweated and carved at the Fleurs du Mal alone with
his ideas and his paper as all artists have worked before
and since.

By-Line: Ernest Hemingway, p. 25

◇

My training was never to drink after dinner nor
before I wrote nor while I was writing.

A Moveable Feast, p. 174

◇

P.P.S. Don't you drink? I notice you speak
slightingly of the bottle. I have drunk since I was fifteen
and few things have given me more pleasure. When
you work hard all day with your head and know you
must work again the next day what else can change
your ideas and make them run on a different plane like
whisky?

to Ivan Kashkin, 1935
Selected Letters, p. 420

[61]

∽

... I have never been a drunk nor even a steady drinker (You will hear legends that I am—they are tacked on everyone that ever wrote about people who drink) and that all I want is tranquility and a chance to write. You may never like any thing I write—and then suddenly you might like something very much. But you must believe that I am sincere in what I write.

to Grace Hall Hemingway, 1927
Selected Letters, p. 244

∽

I haven't been drinking, haven't been in a bar, haven't been at the Dingo, Dome nor Select. Haven't seen anybody. Not going to see anybody. Trying unusual experiment of a writer writing. That also will probably turn out to be vanity.

to F. Scott Fitzgerald, 1926
Selected Letters, p. 217

∽

"Writers should work alone. They should see each other only after their work is done, and not too often then. Otherwise they become like writers in New York. All angleworms in a bottle, trying to derive knowledge and nourishment from their own contact and from the bottle. Sometimes the bottle is shaped art, sometimes economics, sometimes economic-religion. But once they are in the bottle they stay there. They are lonesome outside of the bottle. They do not want to be lonesome. They are afraid to be alone in their beliefs . . ."

Green Hills of Africa, pp. 21–22

❧

All art is only done by the individual. The individual is all you ever have and all schools only serve to classify their members as failures.

Death in the Afternoon, pp. 99–100

❧

"Writing, at its best, is a lonely life. Organizations for writers palliate the writer's loneliness but I doubt if they improve his writing. He grows in public stature as he sheds his loneliness and often his work deteriorates.

For he does his work alone and if he is a good enough
writer he must face eternity, or the lack of it, each day."
Excerpt from Nobel Prize acceptance speech
from CARLOS BAKER,
Ernest Hemingway: A Life Story, pp. 528–529

SEVEN

Characters

～～

MOST of the people in this story are alive and I was writing it very carefully to not have anybody identifiable.

to Alfred Rice, 1953
Selected Letters, p. 820

～

Thanks for your fine letter enclosing the K.C. Star review. I'm so glad you liked the Doctor story. . . . I put in Dick Boulton and Billy Tabeshaw as real people with their real names because it was pretty sure they would never read the Transatlantic Review. I've written a number of stories about the Michigan country—the country is always true—what happens in the stories is fiction.

> to Dr. C. E. Hemingway, 1925
> *Selected Letters, p. 153*

೦

That was the way with Mac. Mac worked too close to life. You had to digest life and then create your own people. Mac had stuff, though.

Nick in the stories was never himself. He made him up. Of course he'd never seen an Indian woman having a baby. That was what made it good. Nobody knew that. He'd seen a woman have a baby on the road to Karagatch and tried to help her. That was the way it was.

> *The Nick Adams Stories, p. 238*

೦

Here is the point. I had a wonderful novel to write about Oak Park and would never do it because I did not want to hurt liveing people. I did not think that a man should make money out of his father shooting himself

nor out of his mother who drove him to it. . . . Tom
Wolfe wrote only of his own life with rhetoric added. I
wanted to write about the whole damned world if I
could get to know it. When I started I wrote some short
stories about actual things and two of them hurt people.
I felt bad about it. Later if I used actual people I used
only those for whom I had completely lost respect and
then I tried to give them a square shake. I know this all
sounds very noble but it is not really horse-shit. The
man [Harold Loeb] who identifies himself as Cohn in
The Sun Also Rises once said to me, "But why did you
make me cry all the time?"

I said, "Listen, if that is you then the narrator must
be me. Do you think that I had my prick shot off or
that if you and I had ever had a fight I would not have
knocked the shit out of you? We boxed often enough so
you know that. And I'll tell you a secret: you do cry an
awful lot for a man."

So now we get back to Oak Park where you feel it
your duty as a scholar . . . to dig into my family while I
am still alive. . . . Nobody in Oak Park likes me I should
suppose. The people that were my good friends are
dead or gone. I gave Oak Park a miss and never used it
as a target. You wouldn't like to bomb your home town
would you? Even if it ceased to be your home town the
day you could leave it?

When you go into my family, etc. it is to me an

invasion of privacy and I gave you the cease and desist. There are defensible interpretations for any violations of ethics or good taste. But I think you will agree that if I had written about Oak Park you would have a point in studying it. But I did not write about it.

to Charles A. Fenton, 1952
Selected Letters, p. 764

✎

Remember Charlie in the first war all I did mostly was hear guys talk; especially in hospital and convalescing. Their experiences get to be more vivid than your own. You invent from your own and from all of theirs. The country you know, also the weather. Then you have a map 1/50,000 for the whole front or sector; 1/5000 if you can get one for close. Then you invent from other people's experience and knowledge and what you know yourself.

Then some son of a bitch will come along and prove you were not at that particular fight. Fine. Dr. Tolstoi was at Sevastopol. But not at Borodino. He wasn't in business in those days. But he could invent from knowledge we all were at some damned Sevastopol.

to Charles Poore, 1953
Selected Letters, p. 800

⌣

I liked it and I didn't like it [*Tender Is The Night*].
It started off with that marvelous description of Sara
and Gerald . . . Then you started fooling with them,
making them come from things they didn't come from,
changing them into other people and you can't do that,
Scott. If you take real people and write about them you
cannot give them other parents than they have (they
are made by their parents and what happens to them)
you cannot make them do anything they would not do.
You can take you or me or Zelda or Pauline or Hadley
or Sara or Gerald but you have to keep them the same
and you can only make them do what they would do.
You can't make one be another. Invention is the finest
thing but you cannot invent anything that would not
actually happen.

That is what we are supposed to do when we are at
out best—make it all up—but make it up so truly that
later it will happen that way.

Goddamn it you took liberties with peoples' pasts
and futures that produced not people but damned
marvellously faked case histories. You, who can write
better than anybody can, who are so lousy with talent
that you have to—the hell with it. Scott for gods sake
write and write truly no matter who or what it hurts but

do not make these silly compromises. You could write a
fine book about Gerald and Sara for instance if you
knew enough about them and they would not have any
feeling, except passing, if it were true.

to F. Scott Fitzgerald, 1934
Selected Letters, p. 407

. . . you ought to write, invent, out of what you
know and keep the people's antecedants straight.

to F. Scott Fitzgerald, 1934
Selected Letters, p. 407

I believe when you are writing stories about actual
people, not the best thing to do, you should make them
those people in everything except telephone addresses.
Think that is only justification for writing stories about
actual people. It is what McAlmon always does and then
he blurs them to make them unrecognizable and not
being an artist he usuallly blurs them to the reader also.

to Ernest Walsh, 1926
Selected Letters, pp. 186–187

⌒

Now watch one thing. In the 3rd volume don't let yourself slip and get any perfect characters in—no Stephen Daedeluses—remember it was Bloom and Mrs. Bloom saved Joyce—that is the only thing could ruin the bastard from being a great piece of literature. If you get a noble communist remember the bastard probably masturbates and is jallous [jealous?] as a cat. Keep them people, people, people, and don't let them get to be symbols. Remember the race is older than the economic system . . .

> to John Dos Passos, 1932
> *Selected Letters, p. 354*

⌒

When writing a novel a writer should create living people; people not characters. A *character* is a caricature. If a writer can make people live there may be no great characters in his book, but it is possible that his book will remain as a whole; as an entity; as a novel. If the people the writer is making talk of old masters; of music; of modern painting; of letters; or of science then they should talk of those subjects in the novel. If they

[71]

do not talk of those subjects and the writer makes them talk of them he is a faker, and if he talks about them himself to show how much he knows then he is showing off. No matter how good a phrase or a simile he may have if he puts it in where it is not absolutely necessary and irreplaceable he is spoiling his work for egotism. Prose is architecture, not interior decoration, and the Baroque is over. For a writer to put his own intellectual musings, which he might sell for a low price as essays, into the mouths of artificially constructed characters which are more remunerative when issued as people in a novel is good economics, perhaps, but does not make literature. People in a novel, not skillfully constructed *characters*, must be projected from the writer's assimilated experience, from his knowledge, from his head, from his heart and from all there is of him. If he ever has luck as well as seriousness and gets them out entire they will have more than one dimension and they will last a long time.

Death in the Afternoon, p. 191

∽

I invented every word and every incident of A Farewell to Arms except possibly 3 or 4 incidents. All the best part is invented. 95 per cent of The Sun Also was pure imagination. I took real people in that one and I controlled what they did. I made it all up.

> to Maxwell Perkins, 1933
> *Selected Letters, p. 400*

◇

Every writer is in much of his work. But it is not as simple as all that. I could have told Mr. Young the whole genesis of The Sun Also Rises for example. It came from a personal experience in that when I had been wounded at one time there had been an infection from pieces of wool cloth being driven into the scrotum. Because of this I got to know other kids who had genito urinary wounds and I wondered what a man's life would have been like after that if his penis had been lost and his testicles and spermatic cord remained intact. I had known a boy that had happened to. So I took him and made him into a foreign correspondent in Paris and, inventing, tried to find out what his problems would be when he was in love with someone who was in love with him and there was nothing that they could do about it . . .

> to Thomas Bledsoe, 1951
> *Selected Letters, p. 745*

◇

I write some stories absolutely as they happen i.e. Wine of Wyoming—the letter one ["One Reader Writes"], A Day's Wait, and another ["After the Storm"] word for word as it happened to Bra, The Mother of a Queen, Gambler, Nun, Radio; After the Storm . . . others I invent completely—Killers, Hills Like White Elephants, The Undefeated, Fifty Grand, Sea Change, A Simple Enquiry. *Nobody* can tell which ones I make up completely.

The point is I *want* them all to sound as though they really happened. Then when I succeed those poor dumb pricks say they are all just skillful reporting.

to Maxwell Perkins, 1933
Selected Letters, p. 400

∽

The only story in which Hadley figures is Out of Season which was an almost literal transcription of what happened. Your ear is always more acute when you have been upset by a row of any sort, mine I mean, and when I came in from the unproductive fishing trip I wrote that story right off on the typewriter without punctuation.

to F. Scott Fitzgerald, 1925
Selected Letters, p. 180

EIGHT

Knowing What to Leave Out

∿

I'VE seen the marlin mate and know about that. So
I leave that out. I've seen a school (or pod) of more
than fifty sperm whales in that same stretch of water
and once harpooned one nearly sixty feet in length and
lost him. So I left that out. All the stories I know from
the fishing village I leave out. But the knowledge is
what makes the underwater part of the iceberg.

from GEORGE PLIMPTON,
"An Interview with Ernest Hemingway"
The Paris Review 18, Spring 1958

∿

I sat in a corner with the afternoon light coming in over my shoulder and wrote in the notebook. The waiter brought me a *café crème* and I drank half of it when it cooled and left it on the table while I wrote. When I stopped writing I did not want to leave the river where I could see the trout in the pool, its surface pushing and swelling smooth against the resistance of the log-driven piles of the bridge. The story was about coming back from the war but there was no mention of the war in it.

A Moveable Feast, p. 76

~

It was a very simple story called "Out of Season" and I had omitted the real end of it which was that the old man hanged himself. This was omitted on my new theory that you could omit anything if you knew that you omitted and the omitted part would strengthen the story and make people feel something more than they understood.

A Moveable Feast, p. 75

~

If a writer of prose knows enough about what he is writing about he may omit things that he knows and the reader, if the writer is writing truly enough, will have a feeling of those things as strongly as though the writer had stated them. The dignity of movement of an ice-berg is due to only one-eighth of it being above water. A writer who omits things because he does not know them only makes hollow places in his writing.

Death in the Afternoon, p. 192

⌒

It wasn't by accident that the Gettysburg address was so short. The laws of prose writing are as immutable as those of flight, of mathematics, of physics.

to Maxwell Perkins, 1945
Selected Letters, p. 594

⌒

My temptation is always to write too much. I keep it under conrtol so as not to have to cut out crap and re-write. Guys who think they are geniuses because they have never learned how to say no to a typewriter are a

[77]

common phenomenon. All you have to do is to get a
phony style and you can write any amount of words.

to Maxwell Perkins, 1940
Selected Letters, p. 501

❧

I . . . threw away about 100,000 words which was
better than most of what left in. It is the most cut book
in the world [To Have and Have Not]. That may be
part of what offends people. It does not have that handy
family package size character you get in Dr. Dickens.

to Lillian Ross, 1948
Selected Letters, pp. 648–649

❧

Ed Hotchner came down last week to see if he
could help me cut the Life material to 30 or 40 thousand
but the best we could do and have it be any good was
around 70. My stuff does not cut well, or even excerpt,
as I cut as I write and everything depends on everything
else and taking the country and the people out is like
taking them out of The Sun Also Rises.

to Charles Scribner, Jr., 1960
Selected Letters, p. 905

❧

As the contract only mentions excisions it is
understood of course that no alterations of words shall
be made without my approval. This protects you as
much as it does me as the stories are written so tight and
so hard that the alteration of a word can throw an
entire story out of key.

to Horace Liveright, 1925
Selected Letters, p. 154

❧

The quail book is monumental, but dull. Eschew
the monumental. Shun the Epic. All the guys who can
paint great big pictures can paint great small ones.

to Maxwell Perkins, 1932
Selected Letters, p. 352

❧

This too to remember. If a man writes clearly
enough any one can see if he fakes. If he mystifies to
avoid a straight statement, which is very different from

[79]

breaking so-called rules of syntax or grammar to make
an effect which can be obtained in no other way, the
writer takes a longer time to be known as a fake and
other writers who are afflicted by the same necessity will
praise him in their own defense. True mysticism should
not be confused with incompetence in writing which
seeks to mystify where there is no mystery but is really
only the necessity to fake to cover lack of knowledge or
the inability to state clearly. Mysticism implies a
mystery and there are many mysteries; but incompetence
is not one of them; nor is overwritten journalism made
literature by the injection of a false epic quality.
Remember this too: all bad writers are in love with the
epic.

Death in the Afternoon, p. 54

◇

    I can write it like Tolstoi and make the book seem
larger, wiser, and all the rest of it. But then I remember
that was what I always skipped in Tolstoi. . . .
    I don't like to write like God. It is only because you
never do it, though, that the critics think you can't do it.

to Maxwell Perkins, 1940
Selected Letters, pp. 514–515

NINE

Obscenity

〜

MADAME, all our words from loose using have lost
their edge . . .

Death in the Afternoon, p. 71

〜

For instance I am guilty of using "swell" in writing.
But only in dialogue; not as an adjective to replace the
word you should use. Try and write straight English;
never using slang except in Dialogue and then only
when unavoidable. Because all slang goes sour in a short
time. I only use swear words, for example, that have

lasted at least a thousand years for fear of getting stuff
that will be simply timely and then go sour.

to Carol Hemingway, 1929
Selected Letters, p. 308

˷

I've tried to reduce profanity [in *The Sun Also
Rises*] but I reduced so much profanity when writing the
book that I'm afraid not much could come out. Perhaps
we will have to consider it simply as a profane book
and hope that the next book will be less profane or
perhaps more sacred.

to Maxwell Perkins, 1926
Selected Letters, p. 213

˷

I imagine you are in more or less of a stew about
certain words but tell me what you can and can't do and
we will work it out. I'm not the little boy writing them
on the wall to be smart. If I can make the effect without
the word will always do so but sometimes can't. Also

[82]

it is good for the language to restore its life that they
bleed out of it. That is very important.

to Maxwell Perkins, 1933
Selected Letters, p. 396

❖

    Here is the piece. If you can't say fornicate can you
say copulate or if not that can you say co-habit? If not
that would have to say consummate I suppose. Use your
own good taste and judgment.

to Arnold Gingrich, 1935
Selected Letters, p. 413

❖

    I imagine we are in accord about the use of certain
words and I never use a word without first considering if
it is replaceable. . . . The whole problem is, it seems,
that one should never use words which shock altogether
out of their own value or connotation—such a word as
for instance *fart* would stand out on a page, unless the
whole matter were entirely rabelaisian, in such a manner
that it would be entirely exaggerated and false and
overdone in emphasis. Granted that it is a very old and

classic English word for a breaking of wind. But you
cannot use it. Altho I can think of a case where it might
be used, under sufficiently tragic circumstances, as to be
entirely acceptable.

to Maxwell Perkins, 1926
Selected Letters, p. 211

◡

The fundamental reason that I used certain words
no longer a part of the usual written language is that
they are very much a part of the vocabulary of the
people I was writing about and there was no way I
could avoid using them and still give anything like a
complete feeling of what I was trying to convey to the
reader. If I wrote any approximation even of the speech
of the bullring it would be unpublishable. I had to try
to get the feeling by the use of two or three words, not
using them directly, but indirectly as I used the Natural
History of the Dead to make a point that you may have
noticed. . . .

My use of words which have been eliminated from
writing but which persist in speech has nothing to do
with the small boy chalking newly discovered words on
fences. I use them for two reasons. 1st as outlined above.

2nd when there is no other word which means exactly the same thing and gives the same effect when spoken.

I always use them spareingly and never to give gratuitous shock—although sometimes to give calculated and what to me seems necessary shock.

to Everett R. Perry, 1933
Selected Letters, pp. 380 and 381

◇

INTERVIEWER: When you are writing, do you ever find yourself influenced by what you're reading at the time?

HEMINGWAY: Not since Joyce was writing *Ulysses*. His was not a direct influence. But in those days when words we knew were barred to us, and we had to fight for a single word, the influence of his work was what changed everything, and made it possible for us to break away from the restrictions.

from GEORGE PLIMPTON,
"An Interview with Ernest Hemingway"
The Paris Review 18, Spring 1958

◇

Green Hills came out in England April 3—Haven't heard yet. They made a very nice looking book. I took out 7 bloodies, one son of a bitch and 4 or five shits voluntarily to see what difference it would make, to please them and Owen Wister. See if it will sail as well or as badly with those reefs. A shame I couldn't have removed a cocksucker as a special gift to Jonathan Cape Ltd.

to Maxwell Perkins, 1936
Selected Letters, pp. 444–445

About the words—you're the one who has gone into that. If you decide to cut out a letter or two to keep inside the law that is your business—I send the copy and you are supposed to know what will go to jail and what will not. F-ck the whole business—that looks all right. It's legal isn't it.

to Maxwell Perkins, 1932
Selected Letters, p. 362

TEN

Titles

∿

WORKING on a title for book of stories now. With
enough time you can always get a good title. The hell
of it is that you always have a lot that seem good and it
takes time to tell which one is right.

to Arnold Gingrich, 1933
Selected Letters, p. 386

∽

How about this for a title
For Whom The Bell Tolls
A Novel
By Ernest Hemingway
. . . I think it has the magic that a title has to have.
Maybe it isn't too easy to say. But maybe the book will

[87]

make it easy. Anyway I have had thirty some titles and
they were all possible but this is the first one that has
made the bell toll for me.

to Maxwell Perkins, 1940
Selected Letters, p. 504

◇

How the hell are you? What do you think of Men
Without Women as a title? I could get no title, Fitz, run
through Ecclesiastics though I did. Perkins, perhaps
you've met him, wanted a title for the book. Perkin's
an odd chap, I thought, what a quaint conceit! He wants
a title for the book. Oddly enough he did. So, I being
up in Gstaad at the time went around to all the book
stores trying to buy a bible in order to get a title. But all
the sons of bitches had to sell were little carved brown
wood bears. So for a time I thought of dubbing the book
The Little Carved Wood Bear and then listening to
the critics explanations. Fortunately there happened to be
a church of England clergyman in town who was
leaving the next day and Pauline brorrowed a bible off
him ... Well, Fitz, I looked all through that bible, it
was in very fine print and stumbling on that great book

Ecclesiastics, read it aloud to all who would listen. Soon I was alone and began cursing the bloody bible because there were no titles in it—although I found the source of practically every good title you ever heard of. But the boys, principally Kipling, had been there before me and swiped all the good ones so I called the book Men Without Women hoping it would have a large sale among the fairies and old Vassar Girls.

to F. Scott Fitzgerald, 1927
Selected Letters, p. 260

◠

Martha is working very hard on her title [*Liana,* 1944]. Getting a title is a lot like drawing cards in a poker game. You keep on drawing and they're all worthless but if you can last at it long enough you always get a good hand finally. She's having a tough time, though, because each year there are fewer good titles since the mines have all been worked for a long time. There are still some wonderful ones in John Donne but two people in the same family become selfconscious about digging into that wonderful lode. So many people have robbed the Bible that nobody minds that and I think we

ought to start Marty digging into Ecclesiastes or
Proverbs where there are still very valuable properties
buried.

> to Maxwell Perkins, 1943
> *Selected Letters, pp. 547–548*

⌒

As for titles I had imagined that I made up A
Farewell to Arms until I read in Capt. Cohn's opus
where I took it from. Same with In Our Time—which
Ezra Pound discovered I lifted from English Book of
Common Prayer—after the box office appeal dies out I
believe A Farewell to Arms will be a good title.
Farewell is about the best word I know in English and
To Arms should clang more than the book deserves—
that title could handle a book with more and better war
in it.

> to Arnold Gingrich, 1932
> *Selected Letters, p. 378*

ELEVEN

Other Writers

I THINK you should learn about writing from everybody who has ever written that has anything to teach you.

to F. Scott Fitzgerald, 1925
Selected Letters, p. 176

Mice: What books should a writer have to read?
Y.C.: He should have read everything so he knows what he has to beat.
Mice: He can't have read everything.

[91]

Y.C.: I don't say what he can. I say what he should. Of course he can't.

Mice: Well what books are necessary?

Y.C.: He should have read *War and Peace* and *Anna Karenina* by Tolstoi, *Midshipman Easy, Frank Mildmay* and *Peter Simple* by Captain Marryat, *Madame Bovary* and *L'Education Sentimentale* by Flaubert, *Buddenbrooks* by Thomas Mann, Joyce's *Dubliners, Portrait of the Artist* and *Ulysses, Tom Jones* and *Joseph Andrews* by Fielding, *Le Rouge et Le Noir* and *La Chartreuse de Parme* by Stendhal, *The Brothers Karamazov* and any two other Dostoevskis, *Huckleberry Finn* by Mark Twain, *The Open Boat* and *The Blue Hotel* by Stephen Crane, *Hail and Farewell* by George Moore, Yeats's *Autobiographies*, all the good De Maupassant, all the good Kipling, all of Turgenev, *Far Away and Long Ago* by W. H. Hudson, Henry James's short stories, especially *Madame de Mauves*, and *The Turn of the Screw, The Portrait of a Lady, The American*—

Mice: I can't write them down that fast. How many more are there?

Y.C.: I'll give you the rest another day. There are about three times that many.

Mice: Should a writer have read all of those?

Y.C.: All of those and plenty more. Otherwise he doesn't know what he has to beat.

Mice: What do you mean "has to beat"?

Y.C.: Listen. There is no use writing anything that has been written before unless you can beat it. What a writer in our time has to do is write what hasn't been written before or beat dead men at what they have done. The only way he can tell how he is going is to compete with dead men. . . .

Mice: But reading all the good writers might discourage you.

Y.C.: Then you ought to be discouraged.

By-Line: Ernest Hemingway, pp. 217–218

§

"All modern American literature comes from one book by Mark Twain called *Huckleberry Finn*. If you read it you must stop where the Nigger Jim is stolen from the boys. That is the real end. The rest is just cheating. But it's the best book we've had. All American writing comes from that. There was nothing before. There has been nothing as good since."

Green Hills of Africa, p. 22

§

". . . we have had, in America, skillful writers. Poe is a skillful writer. It is skillful, marvellously constructed, and it is dead. We have had writers of rhetoric who had the good fortune to find a little, in a chronicle of another man and from voyaging, of how things, actual things, can be, whales for instance, and this knowledge is wrapped in the rhetoric like plums in a pudding. Occasionally it is there, alone, unwrapped in pudding, and it is good. This is Melville. But the people who praise it, praise it for the rhetoric which is not important. They put a mystery in which is not there. . . .

"There were others who wrote like exiled English colonials from an England of which they were never a part to a newer England that they were making. Very good men with the small, dried, and excellent wisdom of Unitarians; men of letters; Quakers with a sense of humor."

"Who were these?"

"Emerson, Hawthorne, Whittier, and Company . . . all these men were gentlemen, or wished to be. They were all very respectable. They did not use the words that people always have used in speech, the words that survive in language. Nor would you gather that they had bodies. They had minds, yes. Nice, dry, clean minds.

Green Hills of Africa, pp. 20–21

◡

[94]

"What about the good writers?"

"The good writers are Henry James, Stephen Crane, and Mark Twain. That's not the order they're good in. There is no order for good writers."

Green Hills of Africa, p. 22

❧

I don't worship Joyce. I like him very much as a friend and think no one can write better, technically, I learned much from him, from Ezra, in conversation principally, from G. Stein . . . Learned a lot from her before she went haywire. Learned nothing from old Ford except mistakes not to make that he had made. . . . Learned from Anderson but it didn't last long. Imitated Ring Lardner as a kid but didn't learn from him. Nothing to learn because he doesn't know anything. All he has is a good false ear and has been around. The poor guy really hates everything but Purity. Learned from D. H. Lawrence about how to say what you felt about country.

to Arnold Gingrich, 1933
Selected Letters, pp. 384–385

❧

I haven't seen Gertrude Stein since last fall. Her Making of Americans is one of the very greatest books I've ever read.

to Sherwood Anderson, 1926
Selected Letters, p. 206

E. E. Cummings' *Enormous Room* was the best book published last year that I read.

to Edmund Wilson, 1923
Selected Letters, p. 105

. . . Miss Stein loaned me *The Lodger*, that marvelous story of Jack the Ripper and another book about murder at a place outside Paris that could only be Enghien les Bains. They were both splendid after-work books, the people credible and the action and the terror never false. They were perfect for reading after you had worked and I read all the Mrs. Belloc Lowndes that there was. But there was only so much and none as good as the first two and I never found anything as good for that empty time of day or night until the first fine Simenon books came out.

A Moveable Feast, p. 27

〜

You are a better writer than Fielding or any of those guys and you should just know it and keep on writing. You have things written that come back to me better than any of them and I am not dopy, really. You shouldn't read the shit about liveing writers. You should always write your best against dead writers that we know what stature (not stature: evocative power) that they have and beat them one by one. Why do you want to fight Dostoevsky in your first fight? Beat Turgenieff— which we both did soundly and for time which I hear tick too with a pressure of 205 over 115 (not bad for the way things have run at all). Then nail yourself DeMaupassant (tough boy until he got the old rale. Still dangerous for three rounds). Then try and take Stendahl. (Take him and we're all happy.) But don't fight with the poor pathological characters of our time (we won't name). You and I can both beat Flaubert who is our most respected, honored master. But to do

that you have to be able to accept the command of a
battalion when it is given. . . .

to William Faulkner, 1947
Selected Letters, p. 624

❧

    I'd no idea Faulkner was in that bad shape and
very happy you are putting together the Portable of him.
He has the most talent of anybody and he just needs a
sort of conscience that isn't there. Certainly if no nation
can exist half free and half slave no man can write
half whore and half straight. But he will write absolutely
perfectly straight and then go on and on and not be
able to end it. I wish the christ I owned him like you'd
own a horse and train him like a horse and race him like
a horse—only in writing. How beautifully he can write
and as simple and as complicated as autumn or as spring.

to Malcolm Cowley, 1945
Selected Letters, pp. 603–604

❧

    Hope this doesn't sound over-confident. Am a man
without any ambition, except to be champion of the
world, I wouldn't fight Dr. Tolstoi in a 20 round bout

[98]

because I know he would knock my ears off. The Dr. had
terrific wind and could go on forever and then some.
But I would take him on for six and he would never
hit me and would knock the shit out of him and maybe
knock him out. He is easy to hit. But boy how *he* can hit.
If I can live to 60 I can beat him. (*MAYBE*)

For your information I started out trying to beat
dead writers that I knew how good they were. (Excuse
vernacular) I tried for Mr. Turgenieff first and it wasn't
too hard. Tried for Mr. Maupassant (won't concede him
the de) and it took four of the best stories to beat him.
He's beaten and if he was around he would know it.
Then I tried for another guy (am getting embarrassed
or embare-assed now from bragging; or stateing) and I
think I fought a draw with him. This other dead
character.

Mr. Henry James I would just thumb him once the
first time he grabbed and then hit him once where he
had no balls and ask the referee to stop it.

There are some guys nobody could ever beat like
Mr. Shakespeare (The Champion) and Mr. Anonymous.
But would be glad any time, if in training, to go twenty
with Mr. Cervantes in his own home town (Alcala de
Henares) and beat the shit out of him. Although Mr. C.
very smart and would be learning all the time and
would probably beat you in a return match. The *third*
fight people would pay to see. . . .

In the big book I hope to take Mr. Melville and Mr. Doestoevsky, they are coupled as a stable entry, and throw lots of mud in their faces because the track isn't fast. But you can only run so many of those kind of races. They take it out of you.

Know this sounds like bragging but Jeezoo Chrise you have to have confidence to be a champion and that is the only thing I ever wished to be.

to Charles Scribner, 1949
Selected Letters, p. 673

❧

"I've been wondering about Dostoyevsky," I said. "How can a man write so badly, so unbelievably badly, and make you feel so deeply?"

A Moveable Feast, p. 137

❧

I've been reading all the time down here. Turgenieff to me is the greatest writer there ever was. Didn't write the greatest books, but was the greatest writer. That's only for me of course. Did you ever read a short story of his called The Rattle of Wheels? It's in the 2nd

vol. of A Sportsman's Sketches. War and Peace is the
best book I know but imagine what a book it would have
been if Turgenieff had written it. Chekov wrote about 6
good stories. But he was an amateur writer. Tolstoi was a
prophet. Maupassant was a professional writer, Balzac
was a professional writer, Turgenieff was an artist.

to Archibald MacLeish, 1925
Selected Letters, p. 179

∽

From the day I had found Sylvia Beach's library I
had read all of Turgenev, what had been published in
English of Gogol, the Constance Garnett translations of
Tolstoi and the English translation of Chekov. In
Toronto, before we had ever come to Paris, I had been
told Katherine Mansfield was a good short-story writer,
even a great short-story writer, but trying to read her
after Chekov was like hearing the carefully artificial tales
of a young old-maid compared to those of an articulate
and knowing physician who was a good and simple
writer. Mansfield was like near-beer. It was better to
drink water. But Chekov was not water except for the
clarity. There were some stories that seemed to be only
journalism. But there were wonderful ones too.

In Dostoyevsky there were things believable and

not to be believed, but some so true they changed you as
you read them; frailty and madness, wickedness and
saintliness, and the insanity of gambling were there to
know as you knew the landscape and the roads in
Turgenev, and the movement of troops, the terrain and
the officers and the men and the fighting in Tolstoi.
Tolstoi made the writing of Stephen Crane on the Civil
War seem like the brilliant imagining of a sick boy
who had never seen war but had only read the battles
and chronicles and seen the Brady photographs that I
had read and seen at my grandparents' house. Until I
read the *Chartreuse de Parme* by Stendhal I had never
read of war as it was except in Tolstoi, and the wonderful
Waterloo account by Stendhal was an accidental piece
in a book that had much dullness. To have come on all
this new world of writing, with time to read in a city
like Paris . . . was like having a great treasure given to
you.

A Moveable Feast, pp. 133–134

◇

Have read Fathers and Children by Turgenieff and
the 1st Vol. of Buddenbrooks by Thomas Mann. Fathers
and Ch-en isn't his best stuff by a long way. Some swell
stuff in it but it can never be as exciting again as when

it was written and that's a hell of a criticism for a book. . . .

Buddenbrooks is a pretty damned good book. If he were a great writer it would be swell. When you think a book like that was published in 1902 and unknown in English until last year it makes you have even less respect, if you ever had any, for people getting stirred up over Main Street, Babbit and all the books your boy friend Menken [H.L. Mencken] has gotten excited about just because they happen to deal with the much abused Am. Scene.

Did you ever read [Knut Hamsun's] The Growth of the Soil? And then for Christ sake to read Thom Boyd . . .

to F. Scott Fitzgerald, 1925
Selected Letters, p. 176

⌒

His own writing [Ezra Pound's], when he would hit it right, was so perfect, and he was so sincere in his mistakes and so enamored of his errors, and so kind to people that I always thought of him as a sort of saint. He was also irascible but so perhaps have been many saints. . . .

Ezra was the most generous writer I have ever

known and the most disinterested. He helped poets,
painters, sculptors and prose writers that he believed in
and he would help anyone whether he believed in them
or not if they were in trouble. He worried about
everyone and in the time when I first knew him he was
most worried about T. S. Eliot who, Ezra told me, had to
work in a bank in London and so had insufficient time
and bad hours to function as a poet.

A Moveable Feast, pp. 108 and 110

❧

I think Tom [Thomas Wolfe] was only truly good
about his home town and there he *was wonderful and
unsurpassable.* The other stuff is usually over-inflated
journalese.

to Maxwell Perkins, 1940
Selected Letters, p. 517

❧

Neither Wilder nor Dos Passos are "good writers."
Wilder is a very minor writer who knows his limitations
and was over inflated in value by critics and as quickly
de-flated.

Dos Passos is often an excellent writer and has been improving in every way with each book he writes.

Both Dos and Wilder come from the same class and neither represents that class—Wilder represents the *Library*—Zola and Hugo were both lousy writers—but Hugo was a grand old man. . . . Flaubert is a great writer but he only wrote one great book—Bovary—one ½ great book L'Education, one damned lousy book Bouvard et Pecuchet.

Stendahl was a great writer with one good book—Le Rouge et le Noir—some fine parts of La Chartreuse de Parme (wonderful) but much of it tripe and the rest junk.

to Paul Romaine, 1932
Selected Letters, p. 366

◇

It is fashionable among my friends to disparage him [Joseph Conrad]. It is even necessary. Living in a world of literary politics where one wrong opinion often proves fatal, one writes carefully. . . .

It is agreed by most of the people I know that Conrad is a bad writer, just as it is agreed that T. S. Eliot is a good writer. If I knew that by grinding Mr. Eliot into a fine dry powder and sprinkling that powder over

Mr. Conrad's grave Mr. Conrad would shortly appear,
looking very annoyed at the forced return, and commence
writing I would leave for London early tomorrow
morning with a sausage grinder.

By-Line: Ernest Hemingway, pp. 132–133

The only reason I can conceive that you might not
want to publish it would be for fear of offending
Sherwood. I do not think that anybody with any stuff
can be hurt by satire.

to Horace Liveright, 1925
Selected Letters, p. 173

[F. Scott Fitzgerald's] talent was as natural as the
pattern that was made by the dust on a butterfly's wings.
At one time he understood it no more than the butterfly
did and he did not know when it was brushed or
marred. Later he became conscious of his damaged wings
and of their construction and he learned to think and
could not fly any more because the love of flight was

[106]

gone and he could only remember when it had been effortless.

A Moveable Feast, p. 147

⌒

He [Fitzgerald] had told me at the Closerie des Lilas how he wrote what he thought were good stories, and which really were good stories for the *Post*, and then changed them for submission, knowing exactly how he must make the twists that made them into salable magazine stories. I had been shocked at this and I said I thought it was whoring. He said it was whoring but that he had to do it as he made his money from the magazines to have money ahead to write decent books. I said that I did not believe anyone could write any way except the very best he could write without destroying his talent. Since he wrote the real story first, he said, the destruction and changing of it that he did at the end did him no harm. I could not believe this and I wanted to argue him out of it but I needed a novel to back up my faith and to show him and convince him, and I had not yet written any such novel.

A Moveable Feast, pp. 155–156

⌒

Work would help him; noncommercial, honest work—a paragraph at a time. But he [Fitzgerald] judged a paragraph by how much money it made him and ditched his juice into that channel because he got instant satisfaction. While if you don't make so much and somebody said it was no good he would be afraid.

to Maxwell Perkins, 1936
Selected Letters, p. 438

∽

The stories arent whoreing, they're just bad judgement—you could have and can make enough to live on writing novels. You damned fool. Go on and write the novel.

to F. Scott Fitzgerald, 1929
Selected Letters, p. 307

TWELVE

Politics

As for your hoping the Leftward Swing etc has a very definite significance for me that is so much horseshit. I do not follow the fashions in politics, letters, religion etc. If the boys swing to the left in literature you may make a small bet the next swing will be to the right and some of the same yellow bastards will swing both ways. There is no left and right in writing. There is only good and bad writing. . . .

These little punks who have never seen men street fighting, let alone a revolution, writing and saying how can you be indifferent to great political etc. etc. I refer to an outfit in, I believe, Davenport, Iowa. Listen— they never even heard of the events that produced the

heat of rage, hatred, indignation, and disillusion that
formed or forged what they call indifference.

Now they want you to swallow communism as
though it were an elder Boys Y.M.C.A. conference or as
though we were all patriots together.

I'm no goddamned patriot nor will I swing to left
or right.

Would as soon machine gun left, right, or center
any political bastards who do not work for a living—
anybody who makes a living by politics or not working.

to Paul Romaine, 1932
Selected Letters, p. 363

◌

. . . don't let them suck you in to start writing about
the proletariat, if you don't come from the proletariat,
just to please the recently politically enlightened critics.
In a little while these critics will be something else. I've
seen them be a lot of things and none of them was
pretty. Write about what you know and write truly and
tell them all where they can place it. . . . Books should
be about the people you know, that you love and hate,
not about the people you study up about. If you write
them truly they will have all the economic implications
a book can hold.

In the meantime, since it is Christmas, if you want to read a book by a man who knows exactly what he is writing about and has written it marvelously well, read Appointment in Samarra by John O'Hara.

Then when you have more time read another book called War and Peace by Tolstoi and see how you will have to skip the big Political Thought passages, that he undoubtedly thought were the best things in the book when he wrote it, because they are no longer either true or important, if they ever were more than topical, and see how true and lasting and important the people and the action are. Do not let them deceive you about what a book should be because of what is in the fashion now.

By-Line: Ernest Hemingway, p. 184

⌒

Now maybe I wrote you this before but will run that risk. You write like a patriot and that is your blind spot. I've seen a lot of patriots and they all died just like anybody else if it hurt bad enough and once they were dead their patriotism was only good for legends; it was bad for their prose and made them write bad poetry.

to Ivan Kashkin, 1936
Selected Letters, p. 432

◡

Now a writer can make himself a nice career while he is alive by espousing a political cause, working for it, making a profession of believing in it, and if it wins he will be very well placed. All politics is a matter of working hard without reward, or with a living wage for a time, in the hope of booty later. A man can be a Fascist or a Communist and if his outfit gets in he can get to be an ambassador or have a million copies of his books printed by the Government or any of the other rewards the boys dream about. Because the literary revolution boys are all ambitious. I have been living for some time where revolutions have gotten past the parlor or publishers' tea and light picketing stage and I know. A lot of my friends have gotten excellent jobs and some others are in jail. But none of this will help the writer as a writer unless he finds something new to add to human knowledge while he is writing. Otherwise he will stink like any other writer when they bury him; except, since he has had political affiliations, they will send more flowers at the time and later he will stink a little more.

By-Line: Ernest Hemingway, p. 183

THIRTEEN

The Writer's Life

"TELL me first what are the things, the actual, concrete things that harm a writer?" . . .
"Politics, women, drink, money, ambition. And the lack of politics, women, drink, money and ambition," I said profoundly.

Green Hills of Africa, p. 28

He [the wolf] is hunted by everyone. Everyone is against him and he is on his own as an artist is.

to Harvey Breit, 1952
Selected Letters, p. 771

❦

Writing and selling it stop but don't get rich stop all authors poor first then rich stop. me no exception stop . . .

telegram to James Gamble, 1921
Selected Letters, p. 45

❦

The one who is doing his work and getting satisfaction from it is not the one the poverty bothers. . . . It was all part of the fight against poverty that you never win except by not spending. Especially if you buy pictures instead of clothes. But then we did not think ever of ourselves as poor. We did not accept it. We thought we were superior people and other people that we looked down on and rightly mistrusted were rich.

A Moveable Feast, pp. 50–51

❦

It is necessary to handle yourself better when you have to cut down on food so you will not get too much hunger-thinking. Hunger is good discipline and you learn from it. And as long as they do not understand it you are ahead of them. Oh sure, I thought, I'm so far ahead of them now that I can't afford to eat regularly. It would not be bad if they caught up a little.

A Moveable Feast, p. 75

❧

Glenway Wescott, Thornton Wilder, and Julian Green have all gotten rich in a year in which I have made less than I made as a newspaper correspondent— and I'm the only one with wives and children to support. Something's going to have to be done. I don't want the present royalties until they are due. But I would like to make a chunk of money at one time so I could invest it. This bull market in beautiful letters isn't going to last forever and I do not want to always be one who is supposed to have made large sums and hasn't and doesn't.

to Maxwell Perkins, 1928
Selected Letters, p. 278

❧

My own experience with the literary life has not as yet included receiving royalties—but I hope by keeping down advances to some day have this take place.

to Maxwell Perkins, 1927
Selected Letters, p. 257

◇

. . . I don't think there is any question about artistic integrities. It has always been much more exciting to write than to be paid for it and if I can keep on writing we may eventually all make some money.

to Maxwell Perkins, 1926
Selected Letters, p. 216

◇

I do not wish to squawk about being hit financially any more than I would squawk about being hit physically. I need money, badly, but not badly enough to do one dishonorable, shady, borderline, or "fast" thing to get it. I hope this is quite clear.

to Alfred Rice, 1948
Selected Letters, p. 655

◇

I've always thought that only one thing mattered,
your own career, and like a general in battle I would
sacrifice anything to my work and I would not let my
self be fond of anything I could not lose. But now I have
learned that you have no success while you are alive;
the only success that counts while you live is making
money and I refused that. So I am going to work for
success after I am dead and I am going to be very careful
of the troops [family] and have no casualties that I can
help and I am going to take pleasure in the things that
I have while I have them.

to Mrs. Paul Pfeiffer, 1936
Selected Letters, p. 436

∽

About posterity: I only think about writing truly.
Posterity can take care of herself . . .

to Arthur Mizener, 1950
Selected Letters, p. 698

∽

". . . You see we make our writers into something
very strange."

"I do not understand."

"We destroy them in many ways. First,
economically. They make money. It is only by hazard
that a writer makes money although good books always
make money eventually. Then our writers when they
have made some money increase their standard of living
and they are caught. They have to write to keep up their
establishments, their wives, and so on, and they write
slop. It is slop not on purpose but because it is hurried.
Because they write when there is nothing to say or no
water in the well. Because they are ambitious. Then,
once they have betrayed themselves, they justify it and
you get more slop."

Green Hills of Africa, p. 23

❧

I get letters from Vanity Fair, Cosmopolitan etc.
asking me for stories, articles, and serials, but am
publishing nothing for six months or a year . . . because
I know that now is a very crucial time and that it is
much more important for me to write in tranquility,
trying to write as well as I can, with no eye on any
market, nor any thought of what the stuff will bring, or
even if it can ever be published—than to fall into the
money making trap which handles American writers

like the corn-husking machine handled my noted
relative's thumb. . . .

to Grace Hall Hemingway, 1927
Selected Letters, p. 244

∾

I cant tell you how glad I am you are getting the
book done. Fashionable thing is to deprecate all work
and think the only thing is to go to pot gracefully and
expensively, but the poor bastards doing this—giving up
their writing etc. to compete with people who can do
nothing and do nothing but go to pot. . . .

to F. Scott Fitzgerald, 1929
Selected Letters, pp. 304–305

∾

Only two things you can do for an artist. Give him
money and show his stuff. These are the only two
impersonal needs.

to Ernest Walsh, 1926
Selected Letters, p. 188

∾

I still need some more healthy rest in order to work at my best. My health is the main capital I have and I want to administer it intelligently.

to Wallace Meyer, 1952
Selected Letters, p. 752

∽

I've been working hard. Had a spell when I was pretty gloomy, that was why I didn't write first, and didn't sleep for about three weeks. Took to getting up about two or so in the morning and going out to the little house to work until daylight because when you're writing on a book and can't sleep your brain races at night and you write all the stuff in your head and in the morning it is gone and you are pooped. But decided that I wasn't getting enough excercise or something so have been going out and driving myself in the boat for a while in any kind of weather and am o.k. now. It is better to produce half as much, get plenty of excercise and not go crazy than to speed up so that your head is hardly normal. Had never had the real old melancholia before and am glad to have had it so I know what people go through. It makes me more tolerant of what happened to my father. But I figure it now that to one who has taken much physical excercise all your life your

body and mind for good functioning need this as much
as a motor needs oil and grease and being in N.Y. all
that time without excercise and then trying to do nothing
but headwork when came back was working the one
part without greasing it with the other. Anyway am
feeling fine now.

to Mrs. Paul Pfeiffer, 1936
Selected Letters, pp. 435–436

∽

The minute I stop writing for a month or two
months and am on a trip I feel absolutely animally
happy. But when you are writing and get something the
way you want it to be you get a great happiness too—
but it is very different; although one is as important as
the other to you yourself when you have a feeling of
how short your life is.

to Ivan Kashkin, 1936
Selected Letters, p. 431

∽

I want to get to Key West and away from it all.
Have never been as damn sick of anything as mention of

this book. People write swell letters about it and I am
so sick of it that a fan letter only makes you embarrassed
and uneasy and vaguely sick. It's hard enough to write
—and writing prose is a full time job and all the best
of it is done in your subconscious and when that is full
of business, reviews, opinions etc. you don't get a
damned thing.

to Maxwell Perkins, 1929
Selected Letters, pp. 316–317

◇

In Piggott [Arkansas] I figure that I will be far
enough away from people so they won't come and
bother and I can work. I will be working on another
novel and some gents when they are working on a novel
may be social assets but I am just about as pleasant to
have around as a bear with sore toenails.

to Dr. C. E. Hemingway, 1926
Selected Letters, p. 207

◇

Write me at the /Hotel Quintana/ Pamplona/
Spain/ Or dont you like to write letters. I do because it's

such a swell way to keep from working and yet feel
you've done something.

to F. Scott Fitzgerald, 1925
Selected Letters, p. 166

⬦

Please forgive the long stupid letters. . . . I write
them instead of stories and they are a luxury that gives
me pleasure and I hope they give you some too.

to Bernard Berenson
Selected Letters, p. xxi

⬦

This letter is sloppy and full of mistakes but is
written in a hurry and is correspondence not an attempt
at prose.

Selected Letters, p. ix

⬦

Take good care of yourself and please forgive such
a rotten letter. All my juice goes in the damned book.

[123]

Anytime I can write a good letter Tubby it's a sign I'm not working.

> to Gen. R. O. Barton, 1945
> *Selected Letters, p. 606*

∽

I hope you have some good fishing this spring. I appreciate your letters so much and am dreadfully sorry I don't write more, but when you make a living writing it is hard to write letters.

> to Dr. C. E. Hemingway, 1923
> *Selected Letters, p. 81*

∽

I miss seeing you and haveing a chance to talk. In talk you can winnow out the bullshit which we put out so pontifically when we write literary letters and we get a good sound understanding.

> to F. Scott Fitzgerald, 1935
> *Selected Letters, p. 425*

∽

Am always a perfectly safe man to tell any dirt to,
as it goes in one ear and out my mouth.

to John Dos Passos
Selected Letters, p. xii

❦

Am writing you only to cool out so please forgive
me. I don't know why people shouldn't write to each
other anyway. They did in the old days. But now I guess
all they want is to be on Television.

to Arthur Mizener, 1950
Selected Letters, p. 697

❦

It is my wish that none of the letters written by
me during my lifetime shall be published. Accordingly, I
hereby request and direct you not to publish or consent
to the publication by others, of any such letters.

to his executors
Selected Letters, p. xxiii

❦

"While Mr. H. appreciates the publicity attempt to build him into a glamorous personality like Floyd Gibbons or Tom Mix's horse Tony he deprecates it and asks the motion picture people to leave his private life alone."

to Maxwell Perkins, 1932
Selected Letters, p. 379

Please do *not* repeat do not put in anything about how many times I have been shot or shot at. I asked both Cape and Scribners not to use any publicity about any military service and it is distasteful to me to mention it and destroys any pride I have in it. I want to run as a writer; not as a man who had been to the wars; nor a bar room fighter; not a shooter; nor a horse-player; nor a drinker. I would like to be a straight writer and be judged as such. . . .

What difference does it make if you live in a picturesque little out house surrounded by 300 feeble minded goats and your faithful dog Black Dog? The question is: can you write?

to Robert Cantwell, 1950
Selected Letters, p. 712

❧

A man can't stay home all the time and when he goes out if anything happens it is in the papers. It is never in the papers that you wake at first light and start working; nor that you serve your country . . . Nor that all the ambition you have ever had is to be the best American prose writer and to work at it hard . . .

to Robert Cantwell, 1950
Selected Letters, p. 709

❧

Lillian Ross wrote a profile of me which I read, in proof, with some horror. But since she was a friend of mine and I knew that she was not writing in malice she had a right to make me seem that way if she wished. I did not believe that I talked like a half-breed choctaw nor that it gave a very sound impression of some one who gets up at first light and works hard at writing most of the days of his life. But I had just finished a book and when you have done that you do not really give a damn for a few weeks. So I did not mind it although I knew it was harmful to me just as the Life piece was. There was

no harm intended and much received. But I am still
fond of Lillian.

to Thomas Bledsoe, 1951
Selected Letters, p. 744

❧

After the New Yorker piece I decided that I would
never give another interview to anyone on any subject
and that I would keep away from all places where I
would be likely to be interviewed. If you say nothing it is
difficult for someone to get it wrong.

to Thomas Bledsoe, 1951
Selected Letters, p. 746

❧

But B.B. I think we should never be too pessimistic
about what we know we have done well because we
should have some reward and the only reward is that
which is within ourselves. . . .

Publicity, admiration, adulation, or simply being
fashionable are all worthless . . .

to Bernard Berenson, 1954
Selected Letters, p. 837

But for reasons which I wrote to Charlie I am
opposed to writing about the private lives of liveing
authors and psychoanalysing them while they are alive.

Criticism is getting all mixed up with a combination
of the Junior F.B.I.-men, discards from Freud and Jung
and a sort of Columnist peep-hole and missing laundry
list school. Mizener made money and did some pretty
atrocious things (to young Scotty and any offspring she
might have) with his book on Scott and every young
English professor sees gold in them dirty sheets now.
Imagine what they can do with the soiled sheets of four
legal beds by the same writer and you can see why their
tongues are slavering (this may not be the correct word.
If not you please supply it).

> to Wallace Meyer, 1952
> *Selected Letters, p. 751*

The writing published in books is what I stand on
and I would like people to leave my private life the hell

alone. What right has anyone to go into it? I say no
right at all.

to Charles A. Fenton, 1952
Selected Letters, p. 765

◇

    I have written the late Mr. Charles Scribner and Mr.
Bledsoe why I am opposed to biography of liveing
writers. There is no use going over that again.

    But do you know it can be damageing to a man
while he is writing in the middle of his work to tell him
that he is suffering from a neurosis as to tell him that
he has cancer? The man himself can say "oh shit." But he
has been damaged with everyone who reads him. And
I have known writers who could be damaged by such
statements to such an extent they could no longer
write. . . .

    But my opposition to public psycho-analyzing of
living people and my conception of the damage this may
do the people is not merely personal. It is a matter of
principle. . . .

    It seems to me, truly, that there are enough dead
writers to deal with to allow the living to work in peace.
From my own stand point, as writer, I have so far had

worry, annoyance and severe interruption of my work
from this book.

to Philip Young, 1952
Selected Letters, pp. 760 and 761

❧

The man [Charles] Fenton is one of those who
think that literary history, or the secret of creative
writing, lies in old laundry lists. . . .

He is now writing about the Toronto period of my
life, and what I have seen of it is completely inaccurate
and silly—last year I spent uncounted hours trying to
help him on his study of my apprenticeship on Kansas
City Star. I could have written three good stories in the
time he cost me. . . .

Dorothy it is a miserable thing to have people
writing about your private life while you are alive. I have
tried to stop it all that I could but there have been many
abuses by people I trusted.

to Dorothy Connable, 1953
Selected Letters, p. 805

❧

I know nothing worse for a writer than for his early writing which has been re-written and altered to be published without permission as his own.

Actually I know few things worse than for another writer to collect a fellow writer's journalism which his fellow writer has elected not to preserve because it is worthless and publish it. . . .

Writing that I do not wish to publish, you have no right to publish. I would no more do a thing like that to you than I would cheat a man at cards or rifle his desk or wastebasket or read his personal letters.

to Charles A. Fenton, 1952
Selected Letters, p. 787

I hold, very simply, that a critic has a right to write anything he wishes about your work no matter how wrong he may be. I also hold that a critic has no right to write about your private life while you are alive. I am speaking about moral rights; not legal rights. . . .

Public psycho-analyzing of liveing writers is most certainly an invasion of privacy.

to Thomas Bledsoe, 1952
Selected Letters, p. 748

⌒

I don't really think of you as a critic—no
disparagement. I mean I think of you as a writer—or
would not make any explanations. Certainly, books
should be judged by those who read them—not
explained by the writer.

to Robert M. Coates, 1932
Selected Letters, p. 368

⌒

Book is truly very good [*Across the River and Into
the Trees*]. You pan it to hell if you don't like it. That
is your right and your duty. But I have read it 206 times
to try and make it better and to cut out any mistakes or
injustices and on the last reading I loved it very much
and it broke my fucking heart for the 206th time. This
is only a personal reaction and should be dis-counted as
such. But have been around quite a while reading and
writing and can tell shit from the other things. . . .

But pan it, ride it, or kill it if you should or if
you can.

to Robert Cantwell, 1950
Selected Letters, p. 711

[133]

〜

For Christ sake write and don't worry about what
the boys will say nor whether it will be a masterpiece
nor what. I write one page of masterpiece to ninety one
pages of shit. I try to put the shit in the wastebasket. You
feel you have to publish crap to make money to live
and let live. All write [right] but if you write enough
and as well as you can there will be the same amount of
masterpiece material (as we say at Yale). You can't
think well enough to sit down and write a deliberate
masterpiece and if you could get rid of [Gilbert] Seldes
and those guys that nearly ruined you and turn them
out as well as you can and let the spectators yell when
it is good and hoot when it is not you would be all right.

to F. Scott Fitzgerald, 1934
Selected Letters, p. 408

〜

Most live writers do not exist. Their fame is created
by critics who always need a genius of the season,
someone they understand completely and feel safe in
praising, but when these fabricated geniuses are dead
they will not exist.

By-Line: Ernest Hemingway, p. 218

[134]

❧

You know lots of criticism is written by characters who are very academic and think it is a sign you are worthless if you make jokes or kid or even clown. I wouldn't kid Our Lord if he was on the cross. But I would attempt a joke with him if I ran into him chaseing the money changers out of the temple.

to Harvey Breit, 1952
Selected Letters, p. 767

❧

Mice: That isn't the way they teach you to write in college.

Y.C.: I don't know about that. I never went to college. If any sonofabitch could write he wouldn't have to teach writing in college.

By-Line: Ernest Hemingway, p. 217

❧

. . . all these guys have theories and try to fit you into the theory. . . . P. Young: It's all trauma. . . . I

suppose when Archie Moore loses his legs P. Young will
diagnose him as a victim of trauma. Carlos Baker really
baffles me. Do you suppose he can con himself into
thinking I would put a symbol into anything on purpose.
It's hard enough just to make a paragraph.

to Harvey Breit, 1956
Selected Letters, p. 867

You know I was thinking about actual sharks when
I wrote the book and had nothing to do with the theory
that they represented critics. I don't know who thought
that up. I have always hoped for sound, intelligent
criticism all my life as writing is the loneliest of all
trades. But I have had little of it except from Kashkin
and from you. Some of yours I disagreed with very much
and others were illuminating and helpful.

to Edmund Wilson, 1952
Selected Letters, p. 793

. . . reading the [reviews] . . . is just a vice. It is
very destructive to publish a book and then read the

reviews. When they do not understand it you get angry;
if they do understand it you only read what you already
know and it is no good for you. It is not as bad as
drinking Strega but it is a little like it.

to Bernard Berenson, 1952
Selected Letters, p. 791

❧

   The chief criticism [of *The Sun Also Rises*] seems
to be that the people are so unattractive—which seems
very funny as criticism when you consider the
attractiveness of the people in, say, Ulysses, the Old
Testament, Judge [Henry] Fielding and other people
some of the critics like. I wonder where these thoroughly
attractive people hang out and how they behave when
they're drunk and what do *they* think about nights.

to Maxwell Perkins, 1926
Selected Letters, p. 240

❧

   Sure, probably I was wrong about the Many
Marriages [by Sherwood Anderson] . . . I will read it
again some time when I can give it a better break.
Reading anything as a serial is awfully hard on it. All

criticism is shit anyway. Nobody knows anything about it except yourself. God knows people who are paid to have attitudes toward things, professional critics, make me sick; camp following eunochs of literature. They won't even whore. They're all virtuous and sterile. And how well meaning and high minded. But they're all camp followers.

to Sherwood Anderson, 1925
Selected Letters, pp. 161–162

⌒

Critics . . . have a habit of hanging attributes on you themselves—and then when they find you're not that way accusing you of sailing under false colors . . .

to Maxwell Perkins, 1926
Selected Letters, p. 240

⌒

About what you say about humor. The bastards don't want you to joke because it disturbs their categories.

to Arnold Gingrich, 1933
Selected Letters, p. 385

⌒

You must be prepared to work always without applause. When you are excited about something is when the first draft is done. But no one can see it until you have gone over it again and again until you have communicated the emotion, the sights and the sounds to the reader, and by the time you have completed this the words, sometimes, will not make sense to you as you read them, so many times have you re-read them. By the time the book comes out you will have started something else and it is all behind you and you do not want to hear about it. But you do, you read it in covers and you see all the places that now you can do nothing about. All the critics who could not make their reputations by discovering you are hoping to make them by predicting hopefully your approaching impotence, failure and general drying up of natural juices. Not a one will wish you luck or hope that you will keep on writing unless you have political affiliations in which case these will rally around and speak of you and Homer, Balzac, Zola and Link Steffens. You are just as well off without these reviews. Finally, in some other place, some other time, when you can't work and feel like hell you will pick up the book and look in it and start to read and go on and in a little while say to your wife, "Why this stuff is bloody marvelous."

And she will say, "Darling, I always told you it was." Or maybe she doesn't hear you and says, "What did you say?" and you do not repeat the remark.

But if the book is good, is about something that you know, and is truly written and reading it over you see that this is so you can let the boys yip and the noise will have that pleasant sound coyotes make on a very cold night when they are out in the snow and you are in your own cabin that you have built or paid for with your work.

By-Line: Ernest Hemingway, p. 185